Managing Projects

Stefan Kühl is professor of sociology at the University of Bielefeld in Germany and works as a consultant for Metaplan, a consulting firm based in Princeton, Hamburg, Shanghai, Singapore, Versailles and Zurich. He studied sociology and history at the University of Bielefeld (Germany), Johns Hopkins University in Baltimore (USA), Université Paris-X-Nanterre (France) and the University of Oxford (UK).

Other Books by Stefan Kühl

Organizations: A Systems Approach
(Routledge 2013)
Ordinary Organizations: Why Normal Men Carried Out the Holocaust
(Polity Press 2016)
When the Monkeys Run the Zoo: The Pitfalls of Flat Hierarchies
(Organizational Dialogue Press 2017)
Sisyphus in Management: The Futile Search for the Optimal Organizational Structure
(forthcoming)
The Rainmaker Effect: Contradictions of the Learning Organization
(forthcoming)

To contact us:
Metaplan
101 Wall Street
Princeton, NJ 08540
USA
Phone: +1 609-688-9171
stefankuehl@metaplan.com
www.metaplan.com

Stefan Kühl

Managing Projects

A Very Brief Introduction

Organizational Dialogue Press
Princeton, Hamburg, Shanghai, Singapore, Versailles, Zurich

ISBN (Print) 978-0-9991479-8-6
ISBN (EPUB) 978-0-9991479- 9-3

Copyright © 2018 by Stefan Kühl

All rights reserved. No part of this publication may be reproduced or transmitted in any form or by any means, without permission in writing from the author.

Translated by: Lee Holt
Cover Design: Guido Klütsch
Typesetting: Thomas Auer
Project Management: Tabea Koepp
www.organizationaldialoguepress.com

Contents

Preface—Managing Projects beyond
the Model of the Organization as Machine.................................7

1.
What Is a Project? A Proposed Definition and Classification 12
1.1 Projects—A Definition 13
1.2 Projects and the Three Sides of an Organization........................21

2.
The Charm and the Limits of Instrumental Rationality in Project Management..28
2.1 The Instrumental-Rational Model of Project Management..........30
2.2 The Function of an Instrumental-Rational Depiction
    of Projects 31
2.3 The Limits of Instrumental-Rational Project Management 33

3.
Project Management beyond Instrumental-Rational Restrictions 37
3.1 Beyond Clearly Defined Project Objectives:
    Contingent Process Management 38
3.2 Beyond the Clear Sequence of Project Phases: Trying
    Things out before Thinking Them through to the End................43

3.3 Beyond Clear Project Evaluations: What Can We Call
    Success or Failure in a Contingent Project Process?..........................47
3.4 Beyond Project Groups and Steering Committees:
    The Dissolution of Classic Project Authorities 53
3.5 Beyond the Win-Win Mythology: Project Management
    as the Organization of Micro-Political Games...................................57

4.
Limits and Opportunities for Management of
Projects Addressing Poorly Defined Problems......................62

Bibliography..66

Preface—Managing Projects beyond the Model of the Organization as Machine

Given the innumerable books on project management, it is worth asking what the benefit of yet another book on the topic might be. There are already several project management books for every niche industry. Various associations and institutes for project management also publish their own manuals. Even the successful For Dummies series offers volumes on *Mindfulness for Dummies* and *Finding a Dream Man for Dummies*, as well as *Project Management for Dummies*, which does not offer anything other than what is in most other project management books (Portny 2010).

The reason for writing another book on project management is simple: namely that there is a striking blind spot in the discussion about project management. The overwhelming number of books, most of the journal articles specializing in project management, and the majority of training courses for project managers are shaped by the notion that you can precisely define a project's goal, determine in advance the resources necessary to attain this goal, and specify in advance a highly detailed project structure for reaching the target, including the assignment of responsibilities.

This approach has a certain off-the-cuff plausibility. It pairs well with the idea that organizations are defined by their purpose, and that the best suitable resources for attaining this purpose must be found. The problem with this perspective, however—

and this has been convincingly demonstrated in organizational research—is that most organizations do not function according to this simple ends-means scheme. Organizations are characterized by contradictory aims that change in frequently unnoticed ways and that cannot be broken down easily into sub-goals for individual organizational units.

This project management book seeks to contribute to a paradigm shift in the management of organizations. The idea that organizations can be managed and optimized like machines may dominate the fantasies of managers and consultants, but the popularity of this notion has suffered significantly in recent decades. It is clear, both from the results of organizational research and from everyday practice, that organizations do not function like simple machines that predictably turn a specific input into a specific output. But even if managers and consultants pay lip service to this reality by describing organizations as "complex," "non-trivial" or "chaotic," the instrumental-rational perspective on organizations still remains dominant in the literature.

This book will show what management and leadership beyond the ends-means scheme can look like. To do this, we begin in Chapter 1 with a definition of projects as a special form of goal programs, and we classify projects within the context of an over-arching organizational perspective, while developing the reasons for the attractiveness of an ends-means scheme in project management. In Chapter 2, we examine the limitations of this approach and then provide an extensive description of an alternative approach to project management. In Chapter 3, we make the case for freeing ourselves from ideas about clearly differentiated project phases, uniquely defined project goals, the establishment of project and steering groups, and the evaluation of projects. In the conclusion in Chapter 4, we assess the opportunities and limits of this alternative approach to project management.

The presentation of our approach relies on several years of experience in working on project management approaches with companies, ministries, administrations, universities, hospitals, and non-profit organizations. Even if this book has emerged out of practical work on project management and is primarily oriented towards practitioners in organizations, I still believe that our approach resonates with insights from scholarly organizational theory. We want to avoid the flaw found in a majority of project management literature for practitioners, namely the lack of reference to specific approaches, such as behavioral decision-making theory, systems theory, or micropolitics.

We can't simplify it too much, though. In management studies we often hear complaints that scholarly texts are difficult for practitioners to put to use, and that texts that are particularly relevant for practitioners typically do not meet the standards of scholarship (Augier/March 2007; Bartunek/Rynes 2014). This text will not be able to fully bridge this gap either. I do hope however that we can situate our proven approach, which I present in detail in Chapter 3, into an over-arching theoretical framework. This audience therefore targets practitioners who aren't scared off by the occasional demonstration of how basic ideas in organizational theory can inform practical recommendations for project management. If scholars find one or another of the book's ideas interesting—such as the classification of projects as a special form of goal program, informed by systems theory—then all the better; but this isn't our primary objective.

This book is part of a small series in which we present the essentials for the management of organizations against the backdrop of modern organizational theories. The *Management Compact* series includes books on the subjects of *Developing Strategies*, *Designing Organizations*, *Influencing Organizational Culture*, *Developing Mission Statements*, and *Exploring Markets*. In our book *Lateral Leadership*, we assess how power, understanding and trust influence the management of organizations. Because we crafted the idea for these books at the same time, attentive readers will notice related trains of thought and similar formulations in all of the volumes in this series. These overlaps were created intentionally to emphasize the unity of the ideas behind the series and to highlight the connections between the volumes.

We do not believe in "simplifying" texts for managers and consultants by crowding our texts with bullet points, executive summaries, graphical presentations of how the text flows, or exercises. In most cases, such "supportive" methods infantilize readers by suggesting that they are not able to draw the central thoughts out of a book without help. That is why in this book, and in all of the other *Management Compact* volumes, we are very sparing with the use of visual aids. Along with a very limited number of graphics, there is only one element that makes reading easier. We use small boxes to introduce examples that give specific instances of our ideas, and we also use them to mark more extensive connections to organizational theory. Readers who are short on time or are not interested in these aspects can skip over the text boxes without losing the thread.

Whoever is interested in empirical research on projects can read *Sisyphus in Management: The Futile Search for the Optimal*

Organizational Structure. You can read more about the theoretical foundations of organizations in my book, *Organizations: A Systems-Approach*, which presents the limits of a machine model of organizations oriented towards an ends-means schema, and an expansive understanding of organizations based on systems theory (Kühl 2013).

This book was developed in the Metaplan training program, "Management and Consulting in Discourse." We would like to thank the participants for their input; they always critically assessed the approaches presented here and brought their practical experiences to the table. We are also grateful to those organizational scholars who have critiqued and commented upon Metaplan's practices in recent decades.

1. What Is a Project? A Proposed Definition and Classification

The idea of a project has been applied to a wide range of things. Couples define the conception and rearing of children as a joint project meant to give their relationship meaning. Hardware stores encourage their customers to "say it with your project," to express their personality by building a new deck in the backyard for grill parties, or to install a new luxurious clawfoot bath tub. Groups of revolutionaries understand their terror attacks as a project meant to change society; it is therefore only logical that the German terrorist group, the Red Army Faction, announced the "end of their urban guerilla project" in 1988 because "this path was not effective in the end." And even Joseph Stalin's idea of doing away with classes by "eliminating non-affiliated or obsolescent classes" has been described by critical observers as one of the "most grandiose projects in world history".

We are not just playing here with the semantic subtleties of the concept of a project; projects are being used, as a structural form, in many different fields of society. In the economy, working on projects that only exist for a specific amount of time has become so important that some believe work in classical organizations is losing its importance. In scholarship, working in research projects has become such a commonplace that some scholars believe that projects are the royal road of the search for truth. In politics, we can see that increasing numbers of citizens may be withdrawing from long-term work in political parties, yet can still be mobilized quickly for projects such as building a bypass road, preventing the construction of public transportation, or blockading international trade agreements. In the context of religion, believers are increasingly turning away from religious organizations and toward project-related religious practice, for example in revival events or religiously themed charity work. Indeed, in the face of such trends, it seems entirely plausible to speak of an increasing "projectification" of society.

But what exactly do we mean when we say project? What characterizes the structural form of a project, which is ostensibly moving forward in society?

1.1 Projects—A Definition

From the perspective of organizational research informed by systems theory, a project is defined as a goal program that should only be performed once. For example, think of the construction of a dam to generate electricity and provide irrigation; the penetration of a new market for rapid transit; the construction of a production facility for computer chips; the creation of a television series; the development of a pharmaceutical product; the preparation of a merger of two universities, or the restructuring of a department.

This definition of projects as one-off goal programs makes it possible to consider projects within the context of a foundational understanding of organizational structure. In systems theory research on organizations, we draw distinctions between three different kinds of organizational structures, or to put it more precisely, premises for decisions (Luhmann 2003). The first set of premises are an organization's *programs*, meaning the decisions regarding if-then programs or objectives through which a member can tell whether he or she has acted properly or improperly. The second set are the *communication channels*, meaning the rights of co-determination, hierarchical authorization to make decisions, and project networks through which communications are governed within the organization. The third type of decisions are those that deal with *personnel*. This understanding of people as a structural feature of organizations may be surprising at first glance, yet it illuminates the fact that staff changes often lead to other decisions, even if communication channels and programs do not change.

The Programmatic Character of Projects

Goal programs—meaning the structural typology relevant to projects—determine which ends or objectives are to be attained. The choice of the means that should be applied to reach the goals or ends remains free within certain limits. Conditional programs, however, are constructed in an entirely different way. They specify what must be done if an organization receives a particular stimulus. Conditional programs therefore have a fixed connection between the condition of an action—the "if"—and the execution of the decision—the "then." The approach is specified with precision: the program determines what must be done—and also implies that whatever is not expressly permitted by the program is prohibited (Luhmann 2003).

Goal programs necessarily entail a reference to time. A goal program to build a municipal airport without a deadline would be destined for failure. It wouldn't even be possible to determine whether the objective was met because the contractors could simply say that they need a bit more time. This would perhaps relieve the responsible parties of their obligations, yet it would run completely counter to the meaning of a goal program. The advantage of programs with a time limit is that it becomes possible, at some point in time prescribed in advance, to determine whether "the objectives have been met or not." The project ends when the objectives are attained or missed (Luhmann 1992, 613).

Even if every project is a more or less discrete goal program, not every goal program can be understood as a project. Goal programs include the installation of a new electrical connection, decisions about the daily menu in a restaurant, or editing a book in a publishing house. Despite the willy-nilly application of the term "project," you would be probably make yourself the laughingstock of your organization if you described the standard laying of an electrical connection, the crafting of today's menu, or the improvement of an author's book as a project.

Goal programs that, as Herbert A. Simon said, approach "well-defined problems," are something that we would probably not call a project. For well-defined problems, the stakeholders involved all agree on the definition of the problem, and it is possible to acquire all of the necessary information about the problem. This enables effective advance programming of task fulfillment (Simon 1997, 128). Sometimes these well-defined problems can be addressed with a conditional program; for example, when adding a new employee to the telephone directory, we use the alphabet and a set of rules to know where to add them. Sometimes, these problems can be treated with simple goal programs for which three or four means are available to choose from.

Consequently, goal programs can be defined as projects only if they address poorly defined problems and if their solutions typically cannot be used repeatedly. We call a problem poorly defined when we only have limited information about its structure, when interpretations of it differ from person to person, and when it is complex enough that it is impossible to weigh all of the alternative solutions and assess their consequences. These kinds of poorly defined problems include for example reorganization projects that have unclear goals or are changed during the project, or complex IT projects that often wind up delivering something other than what was specified in the requirements.

Integrating Projects into Communication Channels

If a goal program has been established to solve a poorly defined problem, then discussions begin within organizations about who is responsible for accomplishing the program. People talk about "creating project structures," "establishing a project architecture," or "setting up project committees." In systems theory, we would say that the project is being integrated into an organization's communication channels. The establishment of communication channels determines how and through what channels official communication in the organization is supposed to travel. By setting up legitimate points of contact, methods of procedure, and responsibilities, the possibilities for communication in the organization are substantially restricted. A large number of possible contacts are put aside, and only a small number of legitimated contacts and decision-making authorities are permitted. Hierarchies and rights of co-determination can be combined in such a way that completely unique communication forms and networks develop.

Projects in organizations are always integrated in some form into the communication channels—and therefore the hierarchy—within an organization. Although people may avoid establishing a project hierarchy within project groups, these groups themselves are enmeshed within the hierarchically arranged communication channels inside an organization. Even in cases in which a project group reports directly to a chairman of the board or a president, it is still integrated into the organization's hierarchy, namely by its direct subordination to the organization's uppermost position. The idea that project work is somehow evidence of a crisis or a harbinger of the end of hierarchies in organizations is naive. In the final analysis, there is hardly a better instrument available for the regulation of non-hierarchical forms of coordination than hierarchy (Kühl 2017).

Depending on the prominence of the projects, completely different forms of organizations can develop. Sometimes an organization is founded for the sole purpose of completing a major project. This was the case for *project organizations* founded for construction projects such as the Stockholm Globe Arena, the Elbphilharmonie concert hall in Hamburg, or Terminal 5 at London Heathrow airport. These project organizations were set up for bids for the Olympic Games, hosting world championships, or organizations for introducing complex development projects, such as introducing a toll system to a country's roads.

In other cases, the core activity of an organization consists of the performance of a number of projects. If we take a look at *project-based organizations* such as consulting companies, engineering firms or advertising agencies, their organizational charts may show supporting functions such as a human resources department, but their core activity is the completion of projects (Hobday 2000). Various terms have arisen to describe this form of organization: "project-based organizations," "project-based enterprises" or "project-oriented companies."

In most cases, a *project* is carried out in an organization *as an exceptional situation*. The core processes of these organizations consist of routine activities, such as the manufacture of bicycles, providing instructional courses, or processing tax returns, but for specific problems—such as the development of an e-bike, a new degree program, or the restructuring of a department—a new structure is created for the project. In organizations in which the implementation of a project constitutes an exceptional situation, it is possible to imagine completely different forms of integration for the purpose of implementing goal programs. For larger projects in particular, members are completely freed up for working in a project group, or are hired solely for the project. In other cases, members from different departments are brought together for a time to work as a project group on implementing a goal program. In yet other cases, project groups are not established at all, and the members are only pulled in to workshops at specific times.

Selecting Staff for Projects

Personnel is the third structure-producing instance in organizations. This is based on the idea that the person (or type of person) who occupies a position makes a difference for future decisions (Luhmann 2000, 221). Attorneys, economists and sociologists would all make different decisions in the same position. People socialized in the upper classes tend to make decisions differently than do people from the lower classes. Organizations have a lot of different ways to adjust their personnel. Hiring a specific person fixes the kinds of decisions that will be made in an organization. Dismissing a certain person can send a signal as to what kind of decisions are no longer wanted in the future. This option is frequently used for top positions to broadcast inwardly and outwardly that other forms of decisions are expected. Internal movement can take the form of promotions, whether as an upward career step or as placement into a sinecure, demotions, as degradation, or to the side. Human resources development is used in attempts to change the behavior of an individual in such a way that he will make different decisions in the same position. This often arouses the impression that personnel represents the "software" of an organization and can be reprogrammed as needed through training, coaching and supervision, while programs, technologies and chains of command constitute the "hardware." The opposite seems to be more plausible. While organizational plans and task descriptions "can be changed easily and practically with the stroke of a pen," people can scarcely be changed (Luhmann 2000, 280).

We can observe how personnel is pressured in and with projects. Attempts to influence the structure of a project through human resource development include internal project management seminars, the financing of project manager training for employees, or the hiring of project management coaches. A variety of companies and institutions have come into being that offer promises to create standards for project management by means of training programs and certifications. Many companies make an effort with these companies and institutions in the hope of being able to establish internal standards through human resources development measures that will lead to greater predictability in project processes. This is why many companies and administrations now offer careers based on projects; people can rise through the ranks from project manager to internally certified senior project manager to externally certified project director.

From a personnel perspective, projects are frequently attractive because they enable seasoned employees (or those who are difficult to fire) to be parked in a project position until something else becomes available. In some companies or administrations, projects are even created for top staff who have to be removed from the leadership of a department. These projects are supposed to keep these people occupied until a new director position opens up, or until they have "cooled off" sufficiently to find a new position outside the organization.

For larger projects, some staff are hired especially for the project and then let go after the project ends. In such cases, staff can be brought on board either through a temporary contract or through service contracts that are awarded for various project tasks. Parts of projects are often outsourced to external service providers. In larger projects in particular, we can see how the hiring and firing of employees represents systematic attempts to influence a project's structure.

1.2 Projects and the Three Sides of an Organization

To understand project management, it is crucial to identify the locations of projects not just in the formal structure, but also to be clear about how the projects can be situated in the organization's informal structure and what role the project plays for an organization's display side. It is only through an understanding of these three sides of an organization—the formal, informal and display side—that we can be able to better assess the significance of projects in organizations.

The Formal Side of an Organization— Fixed Decision Premises

The central feature of organizations is that they can grant membership under one condition: that its members have to accept the organization's expectations. These expectations specify the times at which someone has to be present in the organization's offices, what someone has to do while they are there, which organization members deserve attention and who can be ignored. If someone is not ready to align themselves with these expectations, then they cannot remain a member of the organization. These explicit membership conditions constitute the formal structure of an organization. Formal structures, to put it in a nutshell, are the "fixed decision premises" of an organization.

Most projects are first and foremost anchored in an organization's formal structure. The project's goal—the goal program—is officially announced, and the attainment of this goal is the formal expectation placed on those involved in the project. The project's integration into communication channels is formalized to the degree to which it is expected that both those involved in the project and all other members of the organization have to uphold these aims, at least officially. The assignment of personnel is typically formalized to the extent that a project director or employee cannot simply act as if he or she had nothing to do with the project.

This localization of projects within the formal structure finds expression in the officially promulgated project architectures, network plans, and matrices. To do this, a project is broken down into its intermediate objectives (events) and project steps (processes), and decisions are made about the character of the factual, temporal and social relationships between the intermediate objectives and project steps. This is meant to facilitate not just detailed deadline planning and monitoring, but also the creation of alternative decision paths and planning of buffers for the unexpected.

The Informal Side of an Organization— Non-fixed Decision Premises

In the world of projects, however, things may be much more interesting than what is conveyed by the communicable formal structure, or even the display side presented to non-members. Many aspects of a project are governed through informal expectations; indeed, entire projects sometimes take place within an organi-

What is a project? 23

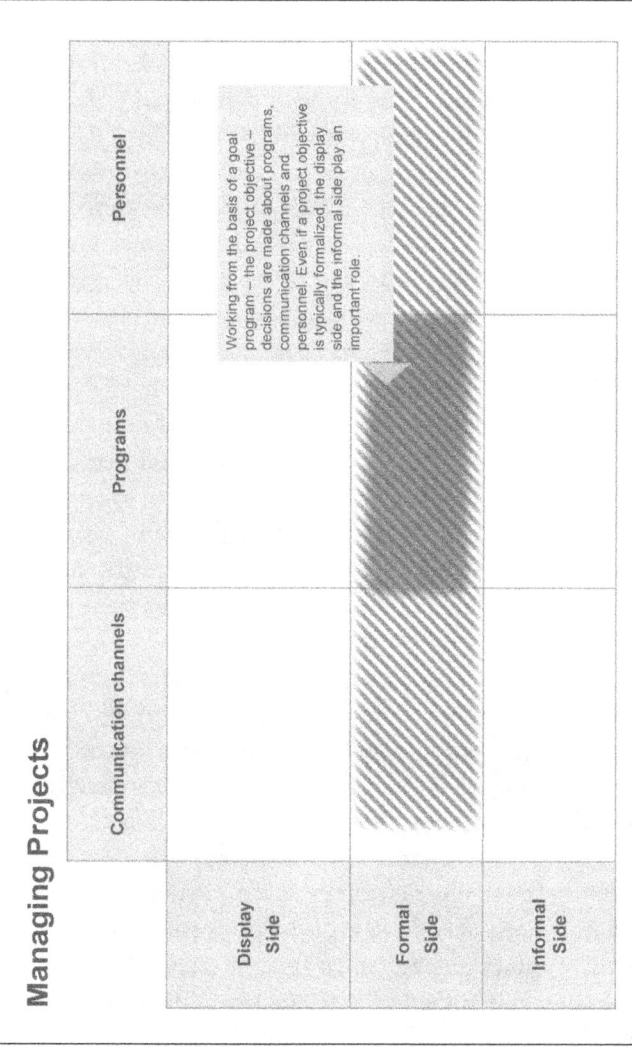

Diagram 1: The structural matrix for analyzing organizations—projects assumed to be goal programs in the formal structure.

zation's informal sphere. By informality we mean the one-time improvisations that blaze a trail through the thicket of rules and regulations, heading off of the network of proven paths that an organization traverses again and again. Informality is about all of the expectations in an organization that *cannot* be articulated in relation to the membership conditions. What these expectations have in common is that decisions were *not* made about them, yet they nevertheless surface as expectations within the organization. Informal structures also have to do with "decision premises," prerequisites that apply to a variety of decisions within organizations.

The non-fixed decision premises—or, to put it differently, the informal expectations—often first reveal themselves in the course of a project when, for example, it becomes clear that there are hidden project goals that were not communicated openly, or that important players outside of the official project architecture are supposed to be kept up to date. These informal expectations are not typically found in the official milestone concepts, network plans, or in the stakeholder analyses.

There are several indications, however, that projects are only able to function at all because they form their very own informal expectations. These informal expectations have little to do with the formation of a project's own culture, which is often romanticized in management literature, even if it is often not about the cooperative interactions in the project that are praised so highly in PowerPoint slides. Instead, the question is rather which informal, and sometimes also illegal, paths can be taken, or how much wishful thinking can go into the description of project steps, and how at the end of the project credit for success and, more importantly, criticism for failure are doled out.

The Display Side of an Organization

An organization's display side plays an important role in project management: presenting a project in the best possible light by means of edited reports, complicated org charts, meticulously detailed process diagrams, and well-crafted press releases. The presentation of the display side involves the creation of a "second reality" that is appropriate for the worlds within and outside of the organization; it has very little to do with the actual processes within the organization. Such project facades do not simply exist; they have to be developed and expanded, regularly maintained, and improved as needed.

EXAMPLE

The Reorganization of Reorganization at a Communications Service Provider

A medium-sized communication services provider has engaged in a fundamental restructuring of operations departments that are spread out over several locations. In the future, the locations themselves will not be the structuring units; instead, organizational units will be structured around major projects implemented across locations. All of the employees on a project being conducted across several locations now report to an account manager who has assumed both the technical and disciplinary management of the employees. The account managers (typically former location directors) now lead teams with about 200 employees who have been reassigned according to their project affiliation. This was done regardless of whether they are stationed in Hamburg, Munich or Zurich. A major campaign by the internal communications department announced the central pillars of this "forward-looking reorganization" with brochures and several major events.

When, after six months, the new organizational structure was not being properly "lived," people found out that the organization had not come very far in emancipating itself from "location-bound thinking." A change management project entitled "stabilizing the new organization" was meant to foster change and provide support for the implementation of new processes. A team made up of company leaders, the human resources department, and operational managers formed a steering committee for the change project, which was led by consultants. To find out where things were going awry, they decided to involve the employees.

In the first project phase, it turned out that central processes were receiving insufficient support from the new organizational design. It quickly became clear that, in addition to a structure based on project affiliation, there still needed to be a location structure that enabled quick reactions to customer requests. This finding met with only limited enthusiasm in the steering committee; after all, the company's leadership and its works councils had campaigned together for the reorganization and had worked hand-in-hand with the employees. Because they didn't want to run the risk of poor results,

> though, the change management project changed its goal over time, becoming less about the implementation of the reorganization and more about the reorganization of the reorganization. To satisfy both critical voices as well as the display side of the company leadership, the project title was changed to "readjusting the reorganization."

There are organizations in which projects are conducted almost exclusively for the benefit of the display side. A project is set up to signal to the outside world that a problem with quality is being addressed, corruption is being tackled, or that gender mainstreaming is being taken seriously. Of course, projects that are conceived primarily for an organization's display side also have to be partially anchored in the formal structure to grant them credibility. Yet because the orientation of such projects primarily serves external appearances, it depends significantly on the fact that the project's display side is heavily emphasized.

2. The Charm and the Limits of Instrumental Rationality in Project Management

At first glance, it seems that almost no field of management enjoys such widespread agreement that there is a "correct approach" more than the accomplishment of projects. Managers, organizational developers, IT consultants and expert advisors are generally unanimous in believing that a project ought to be completed in accordance with "all of the rules of the art." The assumption here is that a prerequisite for a successful project is a precise determination of its goals. A project's specifications manual should describe the objectives with such specificity that one can easily imagine the future envisioned therein, and that the tasks and activities required for attaining the goal are listed there. Classic project management also anticipates the establishment of quantitative and qualitative criteria that can be used to assess precisely the success (or failure) of a project.

According to the predominant tenor in the management literature of the major project management companies, the project should proceed in clearly differentiated phases and steps. Project plans must be produced at the beginning that set dates and deadlines for kick-off events, analysis and diagnosis, data feedback, project conception, presentations, implementation and wrap-up. Despite all of the importance given to flexible adaptation, a central concern remains that implementation should only begin after the diagnosis of problems is finished.

The organizational weapon of choice in project management is the establishment of project teams. The articulation of project aims and intermediate goals leads to a determination of human resource requirements. All of the people needed to implement the project are then identified and brought together into a project team. For more complex tasks, these projects are coordinated and managed by steering committees.

Classic project management literature views disputes about positioning, conflicts of interests, and power struggles as disruptions. They do admit however that conflicts can be indicators for the necessity of changes, reveal opportunities, remove obstacles, promote team spirit, or clear up ambiguities, but in the final analysis they assume that these conflicts can be reduced if everyone involved can agree about the goals and the approach. The idea here is to moderate conflicts in such a way that everyone is pulling together.

An entire "project management industry" has formed in recent years, and this industry propagates these principles of project management (Hodgson/Cicmil 2006). There exist institutes and companies that train tens of thousands of project managers every year in these basic principles. The principles of project management have become so canonical that project managers memorize them for standardized tests given by the Project Management Institute or the International Project Management Association; if they pass the exam, they can receive a qualification as a certified project manager.

The effect is that project work has changed, moving away from a colorful array of project forms that strongly varied even within a company or administration, and moving towards a heavily standardized approach to project management. Project managers are no longer selected merely in an informal way; nowadays people in key positions have to have training in project management, especially in large organizations.

2.1 The Instrumental-Rational Model of Project Management

This notion of project management is based on an "instrumental-rational model" of organizations (Weber 1976, 12), a "mechanistic concept of organizations" (Burns/Stalker 1961, 7). The instrumental-rational perspective always assumes the existence of a "fundamental purpose," which is then viewed as the reason for the existence of an organization. This fundamental purpose, according to an understanding of organizations limited to the instrumental-rational model, can then be disassembled into a multitude of sub-purposes. Following this idea, complex end-means chains can form within organizations; in these chains, every end, or purpose, is only a means for attaining the next end, which for its part is merely a link in a chain of further ends.

In this simplistic understanding of an organization, every purpose, every sub-purpose, and every sub-sub-purpose can be correlated with a position in the hierarchy. The purpose-means structure is aligned in parallel with a hierarchical structure (Weber 1976, 125). Management defines the ways in which an organization seeks to attain its objectives. The actions that are required as a means to attaining an end are "then assigned to subordinates as tasks." These subordinates then "delegate tasks down to lower authorities," until the "bottom of the hierarchy," the level of direct execution, is reached (Luhmann 1971, 96). Ultimately, the hierarchical order of positions would then mirror the "order of ends and means" in an organization (Luhmann 1973, 73).

If every position in a hierarchy is responsible for a specific set of tasks, then, according to this relatively simple understanding of an organization, the position in question need only be filled by an appropriate person. "Select the person best suited for doing the job"; such as the advice of the U.S. expert on rationalization, Frederick Taylor, issued in the early twentieth century (Taylor 1979, 44). At nearly the same time, Max Weber (Weber 1976, 126) articulated the same ideas when he asserted that every task in an organization had to be completed by a "demonstrably successful and trained professional" in order to fulfill the needs of a rational organization.

2.2 The Function of an Instrumental-Rational Depiction of Projects

The appeal of an instrumental-rational view of projects is obvious. Even if the idea that organizations cannot be structured according to a defined supreme objective—a notion occasioned by current scholarly research on organizations and shared by a majority of managers—hope persists among many that—at least for projects—clear goals can be defined, that tools for reaching these goals can be optimized, and that the process for deploying these tools can be scheduled in detail and in advance.

In the *factual dimension*, classic project management assures us that a project's objective is clear. It is then possible, proceeding from this foundation, to begin considering cost planning at the beginning of a project, which then puts the contracting authority in a position to plan projects into his budget. With all of the knowledge about the likelihood of cost deviations, an investment plan, product development or reorganization is then transferred to management's planning horizon in the critical project authorization phase.

In the *temporal dimension*, classic project management assures us that the new construction of a facility or building, the merger of two organizations, or the introduction of a new product can be completed at a defined point in time. Because all of the project's steps have been planned in relation to a precisely defined project completion date, this produces a convincing impression that the project will in fact be finished at the promised time.

In the *social dimension*, the project plan conveys the impression of agreement about targets and approaches. There are stakeholder analyses that examine groups of people who are involved in a project, could be interested in the project's progress, or may be affected by the project. This suggests that project planning has incorporated considerations about the people involved, all with their various interests. Even if graphs and charts of stakeholder analyses, quantitative and qualitative surveys of stakeholder expectations, and impact study spreadsheets assess these different interests, it is still suggested that the project is being developed upon the basis of a compromise between the various participants.

We cannot underestimate the importance of these suggestions in organizations. Organizations seem to depend on receiving such "substitutes for reliability." What politician would approve a building project if they didn't know anything about how it would look and how much it would cost? What company leadership would approve a research budget without having an idea of what will come out at the end? And what developmental aid organization would approve project funding if they were not themselves convinced that this project would have measurable effects at a certain point in time? The reality at the end of a project may wind up having little to do with estimates beforehand, but at the beginning of the project, such self-suggestions seem to be important to the ability to approach a project at all.

2.3 The Limits of Instrumental-Rational Project Management

The promises inherent in project management oriented towards the instrumental-rational model read like a manager's wish list: "shorter project durations thanks to optimized schedule planning," "early detection of dangers and risks," "reduction of cost and effort due to optimized planning," "avoidance of duplicated effort thanks to systematic structuring," "optimal transparence about current and remaining costs," "ongoing cost monitoring through project controlling figures," "optimal distribution of existing capacities," "optimized team qualification through skills management," "error avoidance through systematic project documentation," "standardization benefits thanks to uniform methodology," "avoidance of potential conflicts and efficiency losses," "faster fulfillment of customer requests," "systematic evaluation of innovative proposals," and "faster transformation of innovations into concrete results."

But there are ever more cracks spreading in the shiny surface of classic project management (see for example Packendorff 1995; Maylor 2001; Cicmil et al. 2006). The list of major projects that have failed or been delayed is hard to ignore, such as problems with the A380 wide-body aircraft from Airbus and the 787 Dreamliner from Boeing, the difficulties in the construction of the Stockholm Globe Arena or the Elbphilharmonie in Hamburg, or the problems in building Heathrow Airport's Terminal 5 or Berlin's new airport (Flyvbjerg et al. 2003). If we take a close look at these projects, we will see that they did not fail primarily because of mistakes in the application of classic project management, but rather because of the application of classic project management.

As early as the 1990s, investigations of business process reengineering projects arrived at the conclusion that far more than half of these projects failed (Theuvsen 1996, 73). According to internal studies at a major corporate consulting firm, two-thirds of their proposals failed in the implementation phase (Groth 1999, 52). Examinations of software projects determined that such projects often exceeded their cost limits by a factor of two, that projects went on for twice as long as planned, and that most projects had to go through a reboot at some point during their history (see an early discussion in Lehmann 1979, 115).

Of course, these studies about project failures are always floated to sell new approaches to project management, to offer "project fire department" services for failing measures, or to advertise for better training for project managers. Yet in the face of heavy criticism that extends from the promotion to the rejection of projects, it is hard not to admit that project management is in crisis. The exalted ideals of project management seem to be wearing out over the course of many projects. The longer a project runs, the more contradictions emerge. The stronger a project team is focused on a project's proposed targets, the more obvious the fractures in the proposed target become.

The literature offers a variety of explanations for this disintegration of standards: lack of skills among project participants, truculent employees shaped by Taylorist work structures, a lack of understanding among middle line managers about the project's necessity, a lack of cooperation among organizational, training and IT departments, or the incompetence of consultants. A discrepancy develops between the logical, rational and coherent project management standards and the irrational, emotional behavior of employees.

The problems in a project are blamed on the people involved: "If top management only gave more formal competence to the project director …," "if the project team had been put together in a better way …," "if the participants had only held more intensive discussions …," or "if the consultants only hadn't overseen this aspect …" (Clarke 1999, 139). This personalization of problems makes it possible to uphold the standards of classic project management, even in the face of negative experiences in everyday practice: the plan was great, but unfortunately the people carrying it were not good enough. But this approach cannot satisfy us over the long term.

Classic project management, based on the chronological cycle of defining a problem, analyzing causes, generating solutions and defining actions, fits for the category of "well-defined problems." If a problem can be described in detail, if stakeholders almost unanimously agree on the definition of the problem, and all necessary information about the problem is available, then it makes sense to reach for the instruments of classic project management. If a new water connection is being laid, the problem is clearly sketched (a household wants a water connection), the costs can be defined (the average costs for laying a pipe multiplied by the length of pipe needed), and the work process is clear for everyone involved (according to the work guidelines of the water utility).

Classic project management runs up against its limits in projects in which problems cannot be defined well, for example in tasks that "are heavily influenced by the human factor" and for which "it is not at all clear from the beginning which direction the project should take." Classic project management tools fall apart in reorganization projects because the discovery phase is never clearly concluded, most tasks don't have a clear end, and required resources can only be approximated.

There are projects in which goals and methods are clearly defined (many engineering projects, for example), yet we are often dealing with problems for which the goals are relatively clear but the methods are difficult to define well (e.g., many product development projects), or vice versa, for which the methods are to some degree clear, but the targets aren't right (e.g., many IT projects). Classic project management hits its limits in situations where neither the goals nor the methods are to some extent clear, as in the case of organizational development projects or research projects.

3. Project Management beyond Instrumental-Rational Restrictions

Organizational research has begun to voice doubts about whether projects—as they are described in classic project management textbooks—really ever took place in the reality of organizations. It has been suggested that the descriptions of projects given in management textbooks are merely material for the display side of organizations, thereby maintaining the suggestion that it is possible to plan, predict and control projects.

Instead of holding on to this idealistic notion of an instrumental-rational approach in project management, the following discussion consults current discussions, both in scholarly research on organizations and especially in the management of IT projects, to show what an alternative approach might look like. In the final analysis, people have to find a coherent approach for poorly defined problems. They have to struggle toward solutions, even though they don't have sufficient information or enough time to process the information they do have. They have to proceed, even though the preferences within the organization are unclear, even though they only have vague ideas about the technologies that they should or could use, and even though the group of participants changes constantly (Cohen et al. 1972). In brief: people have to take action, even though they cannot act in a classical instrumental-rational way.

3.1 Beyond Clearly Defined Project Objectives: Contingent Process Management

It is with monotonous regularity that people in projects discover again and again that there are deviations from the plan, in the form of running over on time, budget or staff capacity (interestingly, finishing early, under budget, or with ample staff resources is not seen as a problem). The obvious reaction from the client, project director or project controller is to insist on compliance with the defined framework and to demand greater discipline from project employees with regard to time, budget and capacity.

Going over on time, budget or capacity can serve as an occasion to "improve" objectives. The project team finds out that they cannot use better project management or greater discipline to bring a 25% cost overrun under control, or to address a multi-month delay in attaining a milestone, and so they move the goal posts. The expectations for quality in a software program under development are lowered, the catalog of services for developing a product is reduced, or the demands on the effects of an organizational development project are adjusted.

The more opaque or vague the problem addressed by the project is, the more frequently the attainment criteria must be adjusted by jumping backwards in a logical, linear planning process. The project takes two steps forward and one step back. Development is not steady or constant, and the current step does not offer a foundation for the next developmental step. What forms more often is a feedback loop in which project managers have to go back again and again to revise their plans. These setbacks may lead the project inexorably towards completion, but project planning loses its linear quality. The process becomes highly complex.

Ultimately, a project management approach for poorly defined problems does nothing more than integrate these setbacks into the planning philosophy. The idea behind this kind of project management is to keep the project process contingent. What does contingent mean? Contingency describes the openness of a situation. "It works this way, but also this way, but not just in any old way." An "anything goes" attitude would be a travesty of a contingent process, because the only solution that would be pursued is the one that, at the moment, for certain stakeholders, is seen as favorable. The basic idea of contingency is that there is no "one best way" to approach poorly defined problems; instead, there are various ways forward. The path that is eventually chosen depends on the situation, developments in the organization, power constellations, or random changes in the environment.

This idea draws from findings in modern research on organizations. Management often prefers to try to find the best solution, yet this happens far less often in actual practice than one might think. A group working with the organizational sociologist James March found that a situation often arises in decision-making processes in which solutions "swirl around" in an organization, and these solutions then absorb problems (Cohen et al. 1972). For example, there are expensive machines standing idle in an organization, so people try to think how they could be used in which production steps. Or there is a competent employee who is now underemployed in her original task, so she attracts new job duties. Current ideas about "good management" swirl about through the organization. Hearing about lean management, business process reengineering, or kaizen, managers head out to find problems that might benefit from these methods.

From the perspective of classic instrumental-rational organizational theory, this kind of approach violates all of the professional standards of project management. This kind of approach is referred to pejoratively as "management by muddling through," yet this overlooks the fact that this concept was developed by Charles E. Lindblom after the Second World War as a reaction to the exaggerated fantasies held by administrations and companies (Lindblom 1959, 80). The chief attraction of this "muddling through" concept—or to use a more elegant term, "incrementalism"—lies in finding a management method that is better suited for the reality of an organization than the planning fantasies of classical management (Lindblom 1979, 517).

EXAMPLE

Project Assignment at a Large International Developmental Aid Organization

We can often see this principle at work in the awarding of project contracts. One large international developmental aid organization reports that external consultants spent a lot of time in the hallways because this increased the likelihood of simply being present whenever problems and solutions find each other, and one more actor was sought to head up the project. As Woody Allen once said, "showing up is eighty percent of life."

But even if this developmental aid organization deals frequently with a future association of problems with more or less randomly available actors and solutions, they officially have to act as though—figuratively speaking—the consultants recruited "in the hallways" went through a rigid bidding process. After all, the formal guidelines of this developmental aid organization require them to issue a call for bids for anything over $30,000.

But the professionalism of the organization's project managers is expressed primarily in the crafting of the calls for bids in such a way that consultants who have already been informally selected receive the commission. Of course, this practice on the display side of an organization is contested because it contradicts the organization's own formal guidelines. At the same time, it is the experienced project managers who stand out for their knowledge of how to design guidelines in such a way that an informally preselected solution is formalized.

If we take this seriously, then this has far-reaching consequences for project management: Projects are no longer created once and for all; instead, they are created in a somewhat softer form, to get the project work started—whether the final result corresponds to these objectives or something entirely different is another question. Insufficient clarity for poorly defined problems is no longer understood as a pathology (as in classic project management), but rather as an unavoidable aspect of every project.

What does this mean exactly? To keep a process as contingent as possible, there is only a general agreement about the project's course between the project manager and the "client." The aim here is not to develop a binding formulation of targets and goals, but rather to stake out a framework.

This means that approaches to solutions that already exist in the organization can be integrated into the project whenever the project dynamic calls for it. Elements from the ruins of an earlier software project can be reactivated for projects with a different orientation. Components from a product development process for another client can be recycled. Or the strategic considerations that were discarded three or four years ago during a reorganization, yet remain in the memories of those involved, can offer a "semi-finished solution" for a new problem.

This project management approach resembles that of a bricoleur, or do-it-yourselfer. The project manager proceeds like a hobbyist who tinkers with pieces of solutions that are already available in an organization. The accusation lodged against consultants that they only report on what they found anyway in the company, is from this perspective not an argument against consultants, but rather an expression of their professionalism.

The serious consequences of this approach should not be underestimated. Resources in the form of money, staff and time cannot be derived from project target planning in this model. Yet obviously this kind of approach has to take into account the availability of resources.

The problem with this approach is that holding open a situation in general cannot tolerate the demand for clear goal setting that pervades many organizations as a kind of management mantra. The client, the "master," must therefore on one hand act on the display side as though the project had clear goals and approaches in order to generate the necessary legitimacy, and on the other hand to permit internally the highest possible degree of contingency.

3.2 Beyond the Clear Sequence of Project Phases: Trying Things out before Thinking Them through to the End

The subdivision of a project management into the identification of problems, the development evaluation of alternative solutions, and the implementation of the "best" alternative solution, is still taught in many places as a best practice in project management. A "preliminary evaluation of conceptual possibilities" is supposed to be done first in studies. Then "detailed solution proposals" are developed on the basis of "feasibility and suitability studies." After the awarding of the project, carefully planned in detail, there is then the necessity of ensuring its execution in the form of "implementation," "delivery" or "realization." The project's completion is then marked by "commissioning, handover and takeover."

This approach exists in an idealized form in the waterfall model of project management. According to this model, each project consists of a "cascade" of project phases that are clearly delineated, such as "request," "design," "implementation," "review" and "maintenance." There have to be precisely defined project goals for each of these project phases. Only when the project phase goals, meticulously defined in the technical specifications, are met and documented accordingly in a "milestone meeting" can the next project phase begin (Royce 1970; Benington 1983).

The advantages of this kind of approach emerged in the instrumental-rational model of an organization. This approach structures "the project in delimited, transparent sections of time" and thereby makes "complexity manageable"; it creates "a shared understanding of project management and a uniform approach in the organization"; it reduces the "risk of project execution by defining break points at the phase transitions" at which those responsible can decide whether "a project should be continued or canceled"; and prescribed interim results provide "orientation to employees involved in the project."

Yet in complex projects meant to serve as a solution to poorly defined problems, people often discover in later phases that the solution preferred at the beginning no longer corresponds to the interests and attitudes of important stakeholders. In such situations, setbacks either become necessary, or the project is cancelled because the assigned resources have been exhausted.

Organizational researcher Nils Brunsson (Brunsson 1985) explains this problem as a result of lack of motivational power generated by rational decision-making approaches. The more alternatives that are brought on board, the less convincing the recommendation for action. "We could do it in a completely different way." The more precisely the consequences are examined, the more doubt arises as to whether action is being taken in the sense of the decision. "Should we really do it this way, given all of the dangers?" The more stakeholders who are brought in, the more unlikely it becomes that everyone can be motivated to pursue a specific action.

For projects that approach a poorly defined problem, this problem of motivation can escalate. Because it is not possible to imagine a "right" solution to poorly defined problems, justifiable objections can be lodged against all proposals. As we can see in the seemingly endless discussions in project teams, approach to solutions for poorly defined problems can be doubted to death.

The effect is that people in companies, administrations, hospitals and universities officially strive to uphold rationality in their decision-making, yet in reality they are following other maxims: Only a few people can be involved in a decision. There is a strong preference to only look at the positive effects of a decision. Comparisons are only made with a few alternatives that are obviously inappropriate. Brunsson argues that this approach—which contradicts all of the rules of change management such as participation, precise analysis, or weighing the greatest possible number of alternatives—is the one best suited to generate rationales for action in an organization.

What implications can we draw for project management that aims to solve poorly defined problems?

The maxims of a management approach for projects addressing poorly defined problems are: "Try things out before thinking them through to the end." In software projects, programs are launched before they are designed all the way to the end. It is not at all possible in complex IT projects to think all ideas through to their logical end, or to exhaustively test all of the components. In the development of sensitive products such as medications, companies go into trials before final findings about effects and side effects are complete. In reorganization projects, new rules are tried out and warmed up before evaluating their effects through expert assessments or management workshops.

During the trial, multiple incomplete and contradictory concepts can be kicked off at the same time. It is one of the strengths of organizations that they can hold up under contradictory work methods, opposing strategic goals, and approaches that generate conflict. This considerable ability can also be useful in project management for poorly defined problems because the various strategic thrusts need only be coordinated in a limited way. During the course of trying out various solutions, one approach or another may crash and burn if they do not turn out to be bearable, or they can take on a new quality if implementation seems to promise success. New strategic directions can also emerge during the trial that have not yet been considered.

By labeling these efforts as trials, experiments are shielded off from an organization's normal operations. Because experiments with reform are presented as non-binding, they can be protected, at least partially, against resistance from the organization because it creates the impression that nothing is set down in stone, and everything that is done can be taken back again (Luhmann 2000, 300).

The idea of trying things out is currently popular under several different names. The idea behind "simultaneous engineering" is to allow various developmental steps—which would normally be kicked off one after the other—to begin in an overlapping way. The term "prototyping" describes a process in which a prototype for software, a product or an organizational structure can be brought to trial as quickly as possible, in a space protected from the rest of the organization, without a final determination of which approach to use. "Agile project management" describes the idea of bringing product developments forward in short intervals. All of these concepts do away with comprehensive planning in favor of pushing projects by orienting attention towards iterative interim results.

But this approach has its limits. Sometimes it is not possible to go into a trial because the test setup is too expensive. If we were dealing with an expensive new IT system, for example, this can't be justified internally as a trial and must therefore be planned extensively in advance before going into the testing phase.

3.3 Beyond Clear Project Evaluations: What Can We Call Success or Failure in a Contingent Project Process?

There are often complaints in the literature that projects don't have an official end. People "forget" to hold a project closeout meeting in which the line organization, in the presence of the client, receives the final report about the results, costs and project documentation, thereby officially relieving the project manager and the project team of their duties.

The effect is that project managers often spend years after the project's completion dealing with "aftershocks." Inadequate evaluations also mean that no "institutionalized knowledge production" can be drawn from finished projects.

The problem is also that a lot of time goes by until people can tell whether the project had an impact: did the reorganization project manage to implement a new organizational chart, redistribute competences, or did they just put old wine in new bottles? Can we attribute market success to the product development team's new product, or was it just that market conditions changed for the better? Did the new software project meet with high acceptance among employees, or could we only tell two or three years later that the software is a total shipwreck?

The "official" judgment of projects as successes or failures is often oriented towards the needs of management. A project for introducing an IT project, introducing group work, or the merger of two companies is presented as a success as long as top management can use this for presenting the project to the outside world. If top management changes, it often happens that the same project that was praised as a success is then re-interpreted as a failure to signal a change in the organization's strategic direction. Obviously, the display side of an organization plays a more important role in the evaluation of projects than the formal or informal side.

But despite the orientation of project evaluations to external representation, we should not forget that it can make sense to come to an agreement about the course of a project, beyond the necessity of sprucing up the facade. Even if we are dealing with poorly defined problems in projects, those involved in the project are frequently unanimous about whether or not the project had an impact (beyond the representation of the organization's display side). New rules of the game have developed in the organization; data are now being interpreted differently; dogmas and myths in the organization are being shaken up so that new ideas and action can get off the ground.

The problem with these "successes" is that they often are not (or only partially) anchored in the organization's formal structure. Successes include both major reorganization measures and new informal rules of the game that make it easier for departments to cooperate. Or another interpretation of the data is reflected in the practices of stakeholders, one which enables the growth of new insights and courses of action. Dogmas and myths that formerly restricted stakeholders' thoughts and actions may be unsettled. These dogmas and myths are never formally announced, so when they are shaken up this takes place outside of the formal structure. This is called "organizational learning" in the management literature.

It is important for project employees that projects are protected from critique. It is in the nature of projects that deal with poorly defined problems for goals to fluctuate and for time, money and staffing resources to be nearly impervious to advance planning. For this reason, critics are able in an evaluation meeting to raise an objective that was discussed previously, pointing out that the target was not met. Because there are no clearly defined resources, critics can suggest that the benefit is too slight to justify the expenditure of funds and staff effort.

If a project comes under pressure for these reasons, it may make sense to create success surrogates for the purpose of creating legitimacy: cost savings attained by means of the project are "computed." Revenue increases are attributed to the success of a strategy project, and other possible explanations, for example a market recovery, are ignored.

EXAMPLE

The Legends of Quality Managers, Consultants and Team Leaders

In the French building management company Sommit, there was a great deal of pressure on the board to get problems with service delivery under control after a customer survey revealed criticisms of quality. The board wanted to send a signal to their holding company with a broadly designed kaizen campaign in all of its French teams that it was getting a grip on the quality problem. A task force of experienced staff employees was set up to lead the quality campaign in different teams. The board requested regular reporting from the task force. Several consulting firms specializing in kaizen were hired to support these internal employees. The hope was to stimulate competition among the consulting firms, which would lead to an increase in dedication.

Throughout the entire time, the kaizen campaign was presented to the outside world as a success, and furthermore as a quantifiable one. At meetings between the task force and the board, long lists of improvements were presented and invoices were submitted that showed how the savings outweighed the costs of the kaizen campaign. The pressure to fix the quality deficits led to the production of a "success show" at the end of every single workshop. In response to this demand to present quantified results, on the last day of the workshop there was a joint evaluation of the shortened work processes, the cleared warehouses, and the material savings attained.

The numbers they came up with, however, were only loosely associated with the workshop's results. First of all, savings were quantified in areas in which such quantification was not at all possible due to the complexity of the material. In these cases, people simply asked team leaders for an estimate. Second, successes were attributed to the workshop even if the improvements had already been created previously. Third, there were in some cases very dubious successes. For example, in one workshop, someone tried to create a direct parking spot at a major building so that the unloading times for craftsmen would be shortened. Although all of the participants were aware that this was only a solution created to offset the workshop's time (because there were still long paths to travel at this property), the assessment of success at the end of the workshop resulted in time savings of an entire year, much to the amusement of the participating craftsmen.

How did the workshop's results become so exaggerated? There was no agreement among the participants to sugarcoat the numbers. These success presentations were the result of pressure emanating from the silent body of myths and fictions held by the participating groups. The internal consultants were under pressure to demonstrate the efficiency of their measures so that they could prove their own efficiency in a difficult situation and perhaps even get more people assigned to their task force. The external consultants were under pressure to calculate quantifiable successes in their kaizen workshops so that they could stand out in the competition with other consulting firms. In one consulting firm, it was even standard operating procedure to pay consultants on the basis of the savings they attained in the workshops. For the team and departmental leaders, the kaizen workshops offered an opportunity to present themselves as an exemplary team or branch office. This behavior was encouraged in particular by the fact that the board had announced an internal competition among teams and departments, replete with ranking lists, prizes and awards for team and departmental leaders.

The challenge for project management, despite the impossibility of evaluating crystal-clear project successes, is to embrace something like project learning approaches. This poses a dilemma for project participants because these two processes tend to oppose one another. The presentations of successes prevent learning processes. Admitting to problems or articulating what has been learned often does not fit within the mythological framework of success within projects. There is an art to decoupling these processes in such a way that successes can be presented to the outside world, yet, at the same time, learning processes can take place on the basis of the most realistic project descriptions possible.

3.4 Beyond Project Groups and Steering Committees: The Dissolution of Classic Project Authorities

The literature still describes the establishment of project groups and steering committees as state-of-the-art practices in project management. Experts and process consultants often view these measures as core components of project management. Process consultants who know about group dynamics nurture sympathy for flat hierarchical structures (group work) as a "better alternative" to hierarchical organization. For classic expert consultants it is ostensibly more important to situate their own consultants above project groups, who they equip with their own staff and locate in their own offices.

The establishment of project groups looks plausible at first glance: the management and coordination of groups working full-time on the project is simpler than if new people are constantly being brought on board to the project. The fully responsible group can complete the project more quickly, and then the hierarchy knows where to assign blame if project goes south. If the project group is removed at least partially from the existing hierarchical structure, then there is hope that more innovative solutions will be developed in fixed groups. The establishment of project groups can guarantee that each department can send employees to the project, and external specialists can be brought in.

Organizational research, however, has found that organizations tend to develop special departments for "variations" whose ideas, proposals and concepts are then passed on to "routine specialists" who either carry out implementation in a reluctant way or not at all. Departments for scenario management, for organizational development, or for research and development are responsible for producing knowledge, while operational departments then apply this knowledge. Organizational experts on the staff concentrate on the development of new organizational structures, and the departments integrated in the line are supposed to implement these organizational structures. The establishment of project groups and steering committees is a typical example of differentiation among "variation specialists" whose results are then implemented by "routine specialists."

This frequently leads to an unwanted side effect. If the request for restructuring of company processes goes to special units, then we shouldn't be surprised if all of the other departments withdraw to routine tasks and reject new developments as unwelcome disruptions. This effect can be observed in the "planning ruins" phenomenon: project teams develop IT-supported knowledge management programs that are not used by "users." Strategy groups create new org charts that have not sufficiently taken ruling power structures into account and therefore do not come "alive." Development departments invent new products that later turn out to be completely impervious to mass production.

Steering committees can only help in a limited way to get this problem under control. Steering committees are good insurance against ill-considered reforms (for example, unwanted shifts in power), because such committees are comprised of the people who will later be responsible for implementation. But this comes at a high price. Project teams often expend a lot (perhaps too much) effort in preparing for steering committee meetings; they exhaust themselves with the creation of draft proposals. In some circumstances the proposals are rejected until all of the energy is used up.

When projects fail due to resistance from the line organizations, we could describe this as the "systematic defenses" of a part of the organization that is hostile to innovation, but in the final analysis, these defenses are produced by the establishment of project groups. The project group may distinguish itself with extraordinary speed and creativity in the development of plans, but these effects are neutralized during the implementation of these plans in the everyday business.

Classic project management reacts to this problem by extending invitations for the project team to staff members, external consultants, and as many employees as possible from various operational departments. But this only postpones the problem. If employees from operations are assigned fully to the project, they usually absorb, with surprising alacrity, the logic of consultants and staff positions, which is oriented toward innovation games. If they are only assigned temporarily to the project, then they often view their participation as an onerous duty that keeps them from their "real work."

An alternative to prevailing project management models is the tendency to assign just one project manager as the planning authority who reports directly to the boss. The establishment of project groups or steering committees is largely avoided. In the literature, this approach is described as "influence project management." In this model, the project manager does not have the hierarchical authority to issue instructions to other project participants; instead, he works as a coordinator who consults with participants from the line organizations.

At first glance, the benefit of this approach is that it is no longer necessary to free up staff for a project, and the everyday business flow is scarcely affected for most project participants due to the limited meeting times. The main benefit, however, appears to lie in another aspect. Dispensing with project authorities ensures that the project is not too far removed from the logic of the "routine specialists." What is still more important, however, is that the constantly changing composition of the team should prevent the consolidation of mutually blocking power constellations in the project. The exchanging of staff prevents positions becoming too rigid, too early, in groups. Contingency can be upheld for a relatively long time.

Admittedly, this model runs the danger of having a project manager pushing changes that are inappropriate from the perspective of organizational structures. This risk is mitigated by the fact that workshops and conferences with project participants are always oriented towards reflection, which means that the pros and cons of ideas are weighed against one another.

What are the weaknesses of this approach? Project managers have weak enforcement powers. There is no "authority" in the form of project teams and steering committees to which the project manager can refer. Heavy demands are also placed on the project's sponsor by virtue of their leadership position. He has to ensure support and resources for the project manager. This need not necessarily be seen as a pathology of this model, though. To the contrary: the hierarch remains at the center of all that is happening, and he or she does not have to hand over responsibility to project teams and steering committees.

3.5 Beyond the Win-Win Mythology: Project Management as the Organization of Micro-Political Games

One of the main problems in project management is the burnout among project participants caused by power games and political maneuvering. Descriptions of everyday project work sound like reports from a war zone. There is "trench warfare." There are battles between departments and divisions. In these skirmishes, every department and every division tries to strengthen its own position at the cost of the other's. Project staff develop a "bunker mentality" and "cabin fever," and because they are interested in the project's success, they press into the managerial offices of departments and divisions.

Even if the language used to describe these conflicts assumes overtones of war, we should not forget that these power games result automatically from the interests of various camps. This is not a pathological feature of cooperative relationships; it is an unavoidable consequence of the division of labor. Organizations depend on the breakdown of one task into individual packages that are then completed by different departments, divisions and work groups. The organizational units orient their own calculus to their respective tasks.

If a project is set up in such a way that cooperation takes place between members of a project team, then conflicts result automatically. Each person is in control of a different zone of uncertainty, a field in which only he or she holds required information or access to such information. Whoever is in charge of a zone of uncertainty has power over those project participants who depend on this special knowledge.

When projects deal with well-defined problems, for example the laying of pipe or the production of a telephone book, then we typically see very few power games. This is because the clearness of the problem allows the generation of clear if-then rules for the project's conduct. These if-then rules restrict the development of power games within the project. Projects that seek to solve poorly defined problems do not have these if-then rules that reduce power games.

It is not for nothing that such projects raise questions about the interests about individual stakeholders, such as: what secret aims could the client be pursuing? Is it possible that important people may be relegated to the background, making the whole thing a puppet theater? How great is the danger that someone will try to take unsuccessful prior efforts and advance them under the camouflage of a new name? Are there signs that someone is practicing their alibi in a way meant to prove that the goal was unattainable in the first place? What taboos might there be? Where are the sacred cows hidden? Are there real or supposed "extraneous interests" on the part of the project team or project manager that might have unfavorable effects?

For projects addressing poorly defined problems, management simply has to accept the existence of power games. Everyday conflicts ("conflicts" is another word for power games) in organizations should not be condemned or quickly concealed with efforts at harmony. To the contrary: conflicts, disagreements and power games play a functional role in organizations. The problem is that the set phrases in organizations ("We produce the absolute best cars," "We offer the best service in the hotel industry," etc.) conceal many aspects (for example, "Are our employees trained and able to guarantee top quality?" or "Does the 'best service' cost too much?" etc.). The conflicts between representatives of the different departments, divisions or business units bring these hidden aspects to light and open them up for discussion (Luhmann 1973, 229).

Power games develop in especially powerful ways in projects. Intense friction between the routine games at the foundation of an organization on one hand, and the innovation games among top management and its "variation specialists" on the other, are the order of the day. Günther Ortmann (Ortmann 1994, 65) writes that, at the top of the organization, power games are about strategic goals, modernization and rationalization (innovation games), while middle and lower management in the value-creating departments simultaneously engage in combat over the attainment of the tiniest operational targets (routine games). In projects, these processes, which otherwise run in isolation from one another, collide.

The cards for the next rounds of innovation and routine games are often mixed up in projects. Reorganization projects, product development projects and large IT projects can be understood as meta-games because they are about the rules for future power games. The sophistication revealed by some of the moves in these games are often interpreted, incorrectly, as resistance to the project; yet these moves are not the expression of irrationality, stupidity or laziness; they are instead a phenomenon induced by the organization itself.

How should we deal with power games? In projects dealing with poorly defined problems, it is a mistake to try to solve conflicts as early as possible, or to cut off power games. The project process cannot move forward so long as the micropolitical situation has not been cleared up. A single project meeting hardly offers the challengers and the challenged a chance to get used to one another. To do this, people need time to present and defend their interests, or to give up in favor of a new possibility for action. The maxims of a management approach for projects addressing poorly defined problems must therefore include the prolongation of the project process to allow stakeholders the greatest possible latitude for development.

In a company crisis, it may come to pass that top management asserts themselves in an important project. The "rescue" of Lufthansa by the foundation of the Star Alliance, or the merger of Daimler and Chrysler (at least in the first two years) are stories that have been presented by the media as exemplary instances of strong corporate leadership. In projects that seek to address poorly defined problems, however, we seldom have such a concentration of power in the company leadership. The power resources of the "master" of a project are limited—there are counterparties that see to that. It is therefore important for a project manager to conserve the "master's" power resources, because they could be used up too quickly if he tries too often to deploy it against resistance. One alternative is to set in motion a process of reaching agreement among the participants, because the "master" need not build up a wall of threats at those points where the stakeholders agree.

But beyond the glorification of consensus-finding processes often found in project management literature, we should not overlook the fact that it may be necessary for project managers to resort to the "master's" power. It is precisely because the rationalities of involved actors can be so different that processes of reaching understanding quickly bump up against their limits. In this case, a decree issued by the "master" can help the project to get moving forward again.

4. Limits and Opportunities for Management of Projects Addressing Poorly Defined Problems

The methods for managing projects aimed at poorly defined problems are not a good fit for every project. It's not the right approach for projects with well-defined problems; classic methods of project management are fine for such standard problems. In the final analysis, what matters here is not so much the negotiation of alternative actions than the rapid implementation of ideas. A project with well-defined problems would be inefficient in implementing the methods of a contingent planning process.

The boundary between well-defined and poorly defined problems, however, is blurry. The problem of producing a new telephone book for a company is a well-defined problem because entries do not have to take into account the positions occupied by the employees. The people only need to be listed in alphabetical order, with no regard for their position in the hierarchy. If, however, the telephone book entries have to be arranged according to hierarchy, this can be a poorly defined problem because power interests can embed themselves. The production of a prefabricated home is usually a well-defined problem because all of the uncertainties have been cleared up in advance, and routine programs can be set in motion by precise specifications. Such problems, though, can quickly become poorly defined problems because of unruly contractors, surprise landslides, or the bankruptcies of suppliers. Apparently, more problems deal with poorly defined problems than one might think.

We assume that the approach we describe is very appropriate for everyday work in project management. Goals are formulated in such an abstract way that it is hard to even think of them as vague directions. Despite project management software and phase overlaps, increasing time pressure leads to trials being started without the reflection phase being completed. Finished projects are in many cases not even evaluated; instead, the project participants move right on to the next project in their hectic everyday lives. Power struggles that are very difficult for project managers to get under control are a daily occurrence. The limits of the project team dissolve as additional actors are brought on board, making it impossible to clearly identify who belongs to a project team and who does not.

This reality was long described in the literature as a pathological deviation from proper linear project management logic. Although many project managers influenced by classical teaching admit that projects develop in a much more uncontrolled way than suggested by officially announced project architectures, diagrams and flowcharts, people still cling to their classical project management tools even on projects with poorly defined problems.

It is not easy to break free from this instrumental-rational paradigm because a true "project management industry" has risen up. Whoever wants to make a career as a project manager now has to document their credentials in project management. The large project management companies offer certified training programs. These training courses finish with examinations, much like for accountants, and hardly another form of project management can be better examined than the instrumental-rational paradigm of project management. And because teaching activity in these standardized training courses has become good business for project managers, there is hardly any interest in deviating from this instrumental-rational form of project management (Grabher 2002, 207).

The situation reminds a bit of the famous lock-in example of the QWERTY keyboard. The QWERTY keyboard—the example always given for lock-ins, named after the first row of letters on the keyboard—was considered the best distribution of letters, at the time of its introduction in the mid-nineteenth century, because the sub-optimal arrangement slowed down typists and prevented the type bar from getting tangled up. Although the problem with the type bar no longer applied to computers or optimized typewriters, and another arrangement of letters that would have been more ergonomically efficient was available, there was no change because the costs that would have been incurred by retraining multitudes of employees to the new arrangement would have been too high (David 1985). It is not the most efficient organizational solution that comes out on top; it is the solution that seems most self-evident on the basis of previously made decisions.

Classical project management, oriented as it is towards the instrumental-rational organizational model, is also showing cracks in the public debate. Popular concepts such as agile project management, which by definition eschews long-term goals, does not establish any master plans for projects, and instead sets up multiple competing trials, shows that alternative models are asserting themselves on a larger stage. There is hope that the constant complaint about the discrepancy between project models and project realities is ultimately leading to an approach, even in the education of project managers, that approaches the reality of projects addressing poorly defined problems and that thereby the professional standards for project management will also change.

Bibliography

Augier, Mie, and James G. March. 2007. "The Pursuit of Relevance in Management Education." *California Management Review* 94: 129–146.

Bartunek, Jean M., and Sara L. Rynes. 2014. "Academics and Practitioners Are Alike and Unlike: The Paradoxes of Academic-Practitioner Relationships." *Journal of Management* 40 (5): 1181–1201.

Benington, Herbert D. 1983. "Production of Large Computer Programs." *IEEE Annals Hist. Comput.* 5 (4): 350–361.

Brunsson, Nils. 1985. *The Irrational Organization: Irrationality as a Basis for Organizational Action and Change*. Chichester: John Wiley & Sons.

Burns, Tom, and George M. Stalker. 1961. *The Management of Innovation*. London: Tavistock.

Cicmil, Svetlana, Terry Williams, Janice Thomas, and Damian Hodgson, Damian. 2006. "Rethinking Project Management: Researching the Actuality of Projects." *International Journal of Project Management* 24 (8): 675–686.

Clarke, Angela. 1999. "A Practical Use of Key Success Factors to Improve the Effectiveness of Project Management." *International Journal of Project Management* 17 (3): 139–145.

Cohen, Michael D., James G. March, and Johan P. Olson. 1972. "A Garbage Can Model of Organizational Choice." *Administrative Science Quarterly* 17: 1–25.

David, Paul A. 1985. "Clio and the Economics of Qwerty." *American Economic Review* 75: 332–337.

Flyvbjerg, Bent, Nils Bruzelius, and Werner Rothengatter. 2003. *Megaprojects and Risk: An Anatomy of Ambition.* Cambridge: Cambridge University Press.

Grabher, Gernot. 2002. "Cool projects, Boring Institutions. Temporary Collaboration in Social Context." *Regional Studies* 36 (3): 205–214.

Groth, Torsten. 1999. *Wie systemtheoretisch ist 'Systemische Organisationsberatung'? Neuere Beratungskonzepte für Organisationen im Kontext der Luhmannschen Systemtheorie*, 2nd ed. München: Lit Verlag.

Hobday, Mike. 2000. "The Project-based Organisation: An Ideal Form for Managing Complex Products and Systems." *Research Policy* 29: 871–893.

Hodgson, Damian, and Svetlana Cicmil. 2006. "Are Projects Real? The PMBOK and the Legitimation of Project Management Knowledge." In *Making Projects Critica*, published by Damian Hodgson and Svetlana Cicmil, 29–50. Basingstoke: Palgrave Macmillan.

Kühl, Stefan. 2013. *Organizations: A Systems Approach.* Farnham: Gower.

Kühl, Stefan. 2017. *When the Monkeys Run the Zoo: The Pitfalls of Flat Hierarchies.* Princeton, Hamburg, Shanghai, Singapore, Versailles, Zurich: Organizational Dialogue Press.

Lehmann, John H. 1979. "How Software Projects are Really Managed." *Datamation* 25 (1): 115–129.

Lindblom, Charles E. 1959. "The Science of 'Muddling Through'." *Public Administration Review* 19: 79–88.

Lindblom, Charles E. 1979. "Still Muddling, Not Yet Through." *Public Administration Review* 39: 517–526.

Luhmann, Niklas. 1971. "Zweck - Herrschaft – System: Grundbegriffe und Prämissen Max Webers." In *Politische Planung*, published by Niklas Luhmann, 90–112. Opladen: WDV.

Luhmann, Niklas. 1973. *Zweckbegriff und Systemrationalität*. Frankfurt a.M.: Suhrkamp.

Luhmann, Niklas. 1992. *Die Wissenschaft der Gesellschaft*. Frankfurt a.M.: Suhrkamp.

Luhmann, Niklas. 2000. *Organisation und Entscheidung*. Opladen: WDV.

Luhmann, Niklas. 2003. "Organization." In *Autopoietic Organization Theory: Drawing on Niklas Luhmann's Social Systems Perspective*, published by Tore Bakken and Tor Hernes, 31–52. Kopenhagen: Copenhagen Business School Press.

Maylor, Harvey. 2001. "Beyond the Gantt Chart: Project Management Moving on." *European Management Journal* 19 (1): 92–100.

Ortmann, Günther. 1994. *Formen der Produktion: Organisation und Rekursivität*. Opladen: WDV.

Packendorff, Johann. 1995. "Inquiring into the Temporary Organization: New Directions for Project Management Research." *Scandinavian Journal of Management* 11: 319–333.

Portny, Stanley E. 2010. *Project Management for Dummies*, 3rd ed. Hoboken: John Wiley & Sons.

Royce, Winston W. 1970. "Managing the Development of Large Software Systems." *Proceedings of IEEE WESCON*: 328–338.

Simon, Herbert A. 1997. *Administrative Behavior*. New York: Free Press.

Taylor, Frederick W. 1979. *Die Grundsätze wissenschaftlicher Betriebsführung*, 2nd ed. München: Oldenbourg.

Theuvsen, Ludwig. 1996. "Business Reengineering: Möglichkeiten und Grenzen einer prozeßorientierten Organisationsgestaltung." *Zeitschrift für betriebswirtschaftliche Führung* 48: 65–82.

Weber, Max. 1976. *Wirtschaft und Gesellschaft*. Tübingen: J.C.B. Mohr.

www.ingramcontent.com/pod-product-compliance
Lightning Source LLC
Chambersburg PA
CBHW020303030426
42336CB00010B/886